BRAIN GAMES®

CROSSWORDS

pil

Publications International, Ltd.

Let's get social!
@Publications_International
@PublicationsInternational
@BrainGames.TM
www.pilbooks.com

KEEP YOUR BRAIN FIT!

The fountain of youth exists only in folklore and fairy tales, but that hasn't stopped professionals, laypeople, and everyone in between from attempting to uncover the secrets behind good health and longevity. We all want to stay young and active in order to lead fulfilling lives, but to achieve this, we have to keep our bodies *and* our minds in top shape. How do we do this? Well, there is plenty of information regarding the care of our bodies, but relatively little attention has been paid to the importance of taking care of our minds.

Brain Games® Crosswords is an excellent resource that will help you keep your brain fit for life. With more than 80 crossword puzzles covering a large variety of themes, this book includes puzzles for everyone, from word aficionados to pop culture buffs.

The pleasure of sitting back and doing a puzzle is not only relaxing—it can also help relieve stress after a long day. Whenever you have a chance, turn your downtime into brain-boosting time—and think of the fun you'll have while doing it!

MISHMASH

ACROSS

1. Pretenders

5. Any delightful place

9. Clever comeback

10. Artist's stand

11. Big name in Worcestershire sauce

12. Big name in bikes and keyboards

14. Beetle in Egyptian carvings

17. Threatening talk

19. Wear away, as soil

20. Scapegoat

21. Density times volume

22. Stood up again, as a fallen lamp

DOWN

1. Chef's garnish

2. Bygone Toyota model

3. They don't get deserved acclaim

4. Cohort of Dopey and Doc

6. F.B.I. file, e.g.

7. Invalidates or voids

8. Widely-read book of yore

13. Don, perhaps

15. Like many scifi monsters

16. Watched, as the kids

17. Boiling pot's output

18. Gold brick

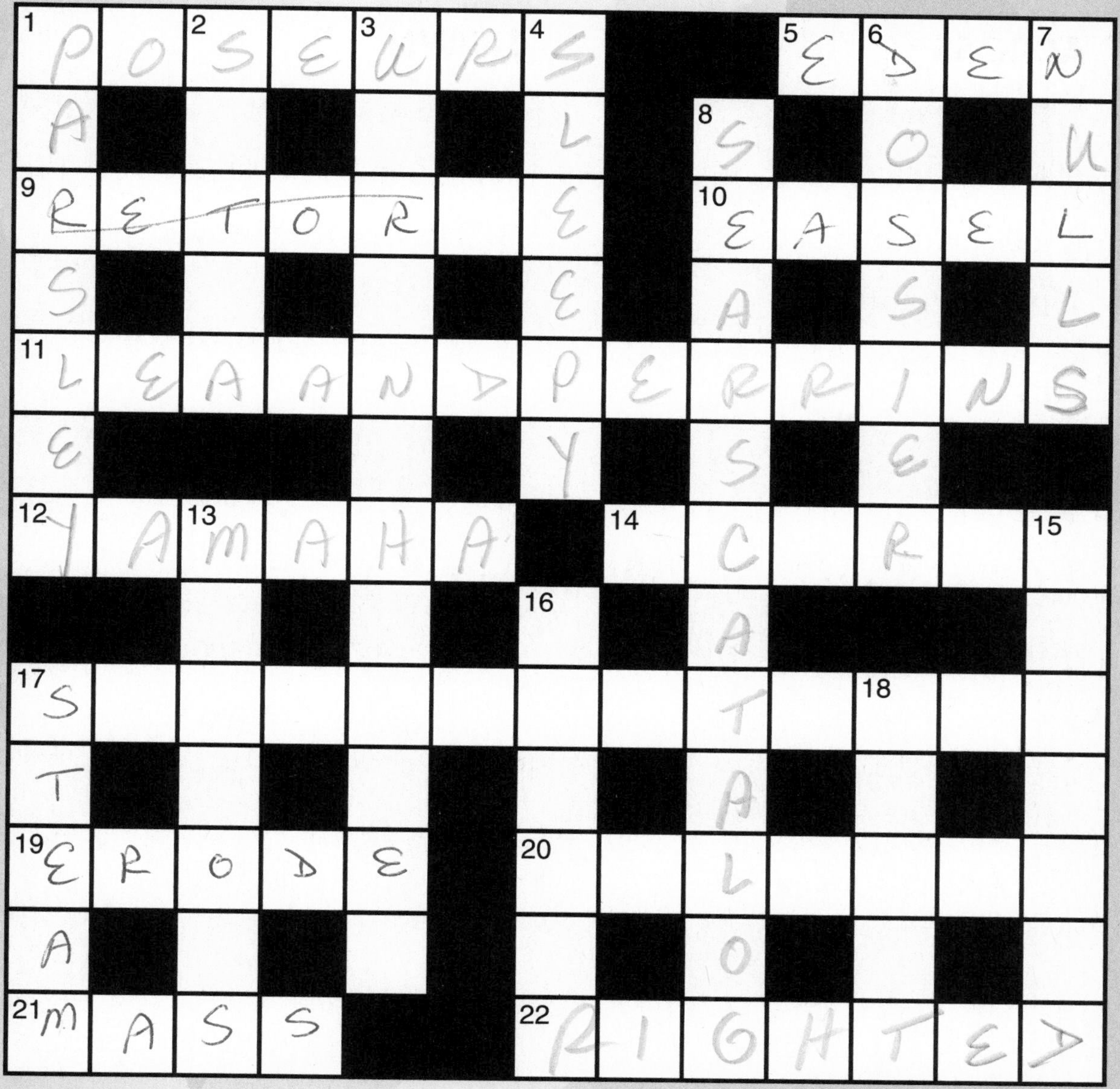

Answers on page 172.

GRAB BAG

ACROSS

1. Discontinue for now
5. Antique photo tint
8. Twist, as a wet cloth
9. Paint diluter
10. Classroom glider
11. Intimate group
12. Like Godot, in "Waiting for Godot"
15. The beginning and the end
18. It'll get you into a lather
19. Kind of typing
20. Crack, as a case
21. Polite social skills

DOWN

1. Clinch, as a deal
2. Casual shoe
3. "The Gold Bug" author
4. Hold for questioning
5. Deserting
6. Chinese bamboo lover
7. See eye to eye about
11. School periods
13. Carry out, as a mission
14. Break the news to
16. Bailey or Buck
17. Aspirin targets

Answers on page 172.

HODGEPODGE

ACROSS

1. Wrist adornment
5. Mischievous little ones
8. Wiggle room, in polls
9. Big-eyed barn bird
10. Devil Dogs, by another name
12. Liked immediately
13. Mingo on TV's "Daniel Boone"
16. Dead-end streets
17. Farrow or Hamm
18. She offered Excalibur to the future King Arthur
19. Greek underworld river
20. "That makes sense"

DOWN

1. Puts in a funk
2. When pranksters come out of the woodwork
3. Miss Manners's bailiwick
4. Huge, in French
6. Walruses and whales
7. Alphabetizes, perhaps
11. Oversees, with "on"
14. Gather, with difficulty
15. Drumming syllables
16. Religious fringe groups

Answers on page 172.

COMMON PHRASES

ACROSS

1. Like machine-gun fire

5. Carries a mortgage, e.g.

8. A bit off

9. Athenian landmark

10. Ones who may dress down those dressing up?

12. Slow, stately dance

14. Tough spot

16. Something bad that has to be done

19. Italian appetizer

20. Aries, in the zodiac

21. "Let it be so"

22. Wet-weather wear

DOWN

1. Bit of lampoonery

2. High points of South America

3. "Licorice sticks," in a band

4. Power perch

6. Up and around

7. Possible perp

11. Getty, for one

12. State with a bison skull on its quarter

13. Knotted attire

15. Place for a mani-pedi

17. Many a September birth

18. 55 or 65, perhaps

Answers on page 172.

RANDOM KNOWLEDGE

ACROSS

1. Clandestine network

5 Bird's roost

8. Words said with a double take

9. Passion

10. Many an agent

12. Our Gang member

14. One under, in golf

16. Story designed to evade

19. Peruvian grazer

20. Nonsense

21. Cavalry horse

22. Soft colors

DOWN

1. Reeled after a punch

2. Crave (with "for")

3. Leading

4. "Mamma Mia!" setting

5. Sitting Bull and others

6. Person called a "carrot-top"

7. Mint, sage or basil

11. Court officials

13. Gonzaga University city

15. Arched foot part

17. Gentle prod

18. "The Sound of Music" setting

Answers on page 173.

TRIVIA

ACROSS

1. Casanova type
5. After-bath sprinkle
9. Bulb from Holland
10. Greek cafe
11. Hypnotizes
12. Father Time's prop
13. The way things are now
16. One whose career is in ruins?
19. Horror-film sounds
20. Greek letter after eta
21. Highest point
22. Squishy chairs

DOWN

1. Ease off
2. "War and Peace" author
3. Colosseum or Hollywood Bowl, e.g.
4. "Maybe even less"
6. "Kiss the chef" garment
7. Aspen Aframes
8. From time to time
12. Doesn't go to bed
14. Home to De Niro's film festival
15. Chocolate dessert
17. About the time of
18. Crocodile ___ (insincere show)

Answers on page 173.

QUIZ TIME

ACROSS

7. Sea-going scientist

8. Without delay

9. Digressions

10. Emulates Lindsey Vonn

12. Sold out

13. Captain Nemo's sub

16. Barreled along the highway

17. "And so on"

19. Garden of Eden exile

21. "It's been ages!"

DOWN

1. "Beat it, kitty!"

2. Cooks in a wok, say

3. Yachtsman or hat

4. Blacksmith's metal

5. Each

6. Fairly long odds

11. Volcanic island near Java

14. Like some Nashville vocals

15. Cleans, as a fish

16. Event for zigzagging racers

18. Everest's continent

20. Becomes ripe

Answers on page 173.

SMALL TALK

ACROSS

1. Sushi wrapper
5. Trench
8. Fleeting light
9. Eyelash cosmetic
10. Color you might see in a nest
11. Gettysburg Address, e.g.
12. Playground period
15. Very special person
18. Thanksgiving offering at many restaurants
19. Bucking horse, informally
20. Chuck Yeager, for one
21. Backwoods valleys

DOWN

1. Mary Poppins' spoonful
2. Cordial
3. Hot-dog-downing event, say
4. Movie maiden "in distress"
5. Dolce & Gabbana, for one
6. Beaten path
7. Doctors and nurses
11. Appears
13. Fine example
14. Surprise attack
16. Laud, as virtues
17. Shaving scrapes

Answers on page 173.

CROSSWORD CURIOSITY

ACROSS

1. Doesn't quite say
5. "Even considering that…"
8. Add to the family, in a way
9. Crimson Tide's school
10. Father, daughter or grand-mother, e.g.
11. Add beforehand
12. Bottomless pits
15. Wild stab
18. Book version
19. Caesar's language
20. Annie's pooch
21. '90s drama about the Reed family

DOWN

1. "I, Robot" author Asimov
2. Advance
3. Nearby
4. Australia has six
5. Sacred insects of old Egypt
6. Baghdad resident
7. These are the people to follow
11. Big pictures
13. "Sleepless in ___"
14. "Beggars Banquet" band, briefly
16. Bermuda or Vidalia
17. Sovereigns

Answers on page 174.

GENERAL KNOWLEDGE

ACROSS

1. Bro-ey greeting
5. Gator's counterpart
9. Desktop receptacle
10. One-named Barbadian singer
11. Sports-bar fare often served with ranch dip
13. Confer holy orders on
14. Aphrodite's lover
17. "Little Miss Muffet," e.g.
20. Cause of handwringing
21. Engage in swordplay
22. No, to Putin
23. Per se

DOWN

1. Aluminum sheet in the kitchen
2. Inhibited
3. What "Boffo" means in Variety
4. Esprit de corps
6. Minor altercation
7. Least refined
8. Gabbed
12. Trevi attraction
15. Award hopeful
16. Boa relative
18. Elephant gone amok
19. Cut made by a saw

Answers on page 174.

MELANGE

ACROSS

7. Size for the slender
8. Connect to an outlet
9. Brazen
10. Grotesque imitation
11. Diplomatic messenger
13. Towel fabric
15. "Greetings!"
17. Venus ___ (bug-eating plant)
20. Routine
21. Lotus position discipline
23. Cash in, as chips
24. Hardy's "The Return of the ___"

DOWN

1. It's nothing, really
2. Auction participant
3. "Strawberry Fields Forever" band
4. Atomizer mist
5. Dramatist O'Neill
6. Africa's largest lake
12. Survey or summary
14. Actively in a game
16. Of greater size
18. Tundra maker
19. Second or sixth President
22. Be charitable

Answers on page 174.

QUIZ SHOW

ACROSS

1. Pedicab kin
5. Bee Gees family name
9. Crown jewels repository
10. Mentor's charge
11. Chinos color
12. Least fatty cooking oil
13. Slender, graceful girls
16. Boots out
18. Counting everything
20. "See you again!"
21. Bit of fishing gear
22. They make arrangements

DOWN

1. Pave over, as a driveway
2. Provincial place
3. Like Dali's art
4. Butler at Wayne Manor
6. "Slumdog Millionaire" country
7. Desperados
8. Duck or Shark
12. Clam soup
14. Irrational fears
15. Nadal of tennis
17. Hill on Vail
19. Least desirable parts

Answers on page 174.

CLUE COLLECTION

ACROSS

1. Sort of strange

4. Big money maker

9. End of the train

10. Amtrak highspeed train

11. Sweetheart, child or pet, perhaps

12. Seashore building projects

17. Ponzi's plan

20. Breakfast treat, informally

21. Garb

22. Cleaner for gun barrels

23. Kutcher of "Two and a Half Men"

DOWN

1. Available, as a physician

2. Clean up, as code

3. Did some reconnaissance

5. Disreputable

6. Beatles song on "Let It Be"

7. Brief trailer

8. Homer Simpson's neighbor

13. Radar or scuba, e.g.

14. Computer geeks, e.g.

15. Black widow, for one

16. "Annie Hall" star

18. "Be Prepared," e.g.

19. Chicago Sun-Times critic Roger

Answers on page 175.

ODDMENTS

ACROSS

1. Racetrack tout
5. Amulet
8. Mario's dinosaur pal
9. Entranceway employee
10. Tall tale
11. Play ___ (feign death)
12. Pilgrim's destination
15. Accepts consequences
18. Dodgy
19. "The bombs bursting ___"
20. Gold rush territory
21. "Inner" holy place

DOWN

1. "Happy birthday ___!"
2. Pulverizing tools
3. "How many months have 28 days?," e.g.
4. Entertain lavishly
5. Kasparov or Fischer
6. Houston player
7. Words with a nice ring to them?
11. Hype
13. Word before coffee or replay
14. Bed linens
16. Metal-on-metal sound
17. Billiard ball bounce

Answers on page 175.

MISCELLANY

ACROSS

1. Angel hair or elbows
4. Cut into thirds
7. Biblical land of many tongues
8. Colorful candies
9. Sibling of Aaron and Miriam
11. Ottoman, e.g.
15. Audacious adventure
17. Athos, Porthos and Aramis, e.g.
19. Simmons product
20. Form of passive protest
21. Pretended to be
22. All-too-public spat

DOWN

1. Beat around the bush
2. Audited, as a college class
3. Lacking ornament
4. Driven personalities
5. Haifa hello
6. Domain of King Minos
10. Incidental discussion point
12. Unnerves
13. Word in some newspaper names
14. "Don Quixote" or "Gulliver's Travels"
16. Barrel slats
18. Horned herbivore

Answers on page 175.

MANY M'S

ACROSS

1. Car that does 185 in "Life's Been Good"
6. Paydirt, in football
9. Hard on the ears
10. Badly rattled
11. Lined up
15. Utilized fully
16. High point of Holy Week?
20. Really hate
21. Lacking a brand name
23. After taxes
24. Hard to take
25. Didn't stop

DOWN

1. Adherent of Islam
2. Array of food
3. All the rage
4. Change for a hundred
5. Up for it
7. Hepcat's attire
8. Personality problems
12. Emperor exiled to Elba
13. Santa's team
14. Celebrate in a big way
17. Brings to the ground
18. Killed in the Oval Office
19. Coldly determined
22. Diego's dwelling

Answers on page 175.

IN THE BOOKS

ACROSS

1. Cast a spell over

5. In actuality

9. Making charged particles

10. Cravat pin

11. Grammatical glitch

12. Firmly fixed

15. Fundamental right of governments

18. Baby's bear

19. SmackDown figure

21. Thoroughly memorized

22. Like an Oreo cookie, visually

23. Bad-mouth

24. Hue of Dorothy's slippers in Oz

DOWN

1. Egyptian funerary text

2. Super-intense

3. Caribbean island

4. Political dominance

6. "8 Mile" rapper

7. Film director's cry

8. Behavioral quirks

12. Desalinization input

13. Highly volatile situation

14. A house away

16. "Yellow Submarine" villain

17. Baggage attachments

20. Fishing poles

Answers on page 176.

IN PRINT

ACROSS

7. Exactly so

8. Like Laundromat washers, for short

9. Where to buy Time

11. "But of course!"

13. "Let's see here..."

15. Dance orchestra

17. Benton of "Hee Haw"

19. Of like mind

21. Arrive unnoticed

22. Give back

DOWN

1. Fat Man or Little Boy

2. Villain in the story

3. A French city, not a team

4. Old name of a group that now includes girls

5. Beyond sore

6. Common tater

10. Brainstorming product, hopefully

12. Dubious remedy

14. Candidates not on ballots

16. "Get busy!"

18. Do research

19. Banish from office

20. Adam and Eve's first home

Answers on page 176.

TWO FROM MYTHOLOGY

ACROSS

7. Face, as a judge

8. Walk on a trail

9. Gets ready to drag

10. Mole, for example

11. Vulnerable point

15. Mythical fountain's reward

16. Top 40 songs, for example

19. Bullets, pellets, et al.

21. Roll call answer

22. Nonverbal welcome

DOWN

1. Draw near

2. Choose to ignore

3. Barrel diameter

4. Business setback

5. "Holy cow!"

6. Army chaplain, informally

12. Think deeply about

13. Likely loser

14. WWII bomber

17. Earth inheritor, per Matthew

18. Did a prompter's job

20. Baby doll cry

Answers on page 176.

SMORGASBORD

ACROSS

1. Without a cent
6. Gives lessons
7. Consumed greedily
9. "The Flintstones" wife
10. Hooter with a home
11. It's upper case
14. Before you know it
16. Game show host
18. Beanie top
19. He played Lou Grant
20. Mythical arrow shooter

DOWN

1. Easily damaged
2. Deep down
3. Diamond of sports
4. Broadcast studio alert
5. Barely makes
6. News spreader of long ago
8. Arctic dweller with a white coat
12. Credit card material
13. Young female sheep
15. "Let ___!" ("Go ahead!")
17. Reba's realm, for short

Answers on page 176.

FRIENDSHIP AND FIRE

ACROSS

1. Childcare worker
4. "Count on it!"
8. April Fools' Day prank, perhaps
10. Lopsided victory
11. "Catch ya later!"
12. Flowering
16. "Bless you!" prompter
17. About 1520 miles per hour
19. Be loyal to each other
20. Bad traffic jams
21. Passes, as time

DOWN

1. Bobbing targets
2. Tempts fate
3. Dragged behind
5. Offshore drillers
6. Lighter alternative
7. Drive at Pebble Beach
9. Follow as a model
13. Obstruct
14. Bothers persistently
15. Cocktail or a Scottish hero
18. System of belief

Answers on page 177.

METAL AND CLOTH

ACROSS

7. Got the crowd going

9. "Ben-Hur" costume

10. Garment that reveals the knees

11. Bed covering

12. Connect with

14. Controversial tennis star John

16. Athlete's TV greeting

18. Jalopy

21. Elite Special Forces force

22. After a bit

DOWN

1. Eat a lot of pasta, with "up"

2. Fire up

3. Recording device

4. Allergic reaction

5. Circumvention

6. Common power outage cause

8. Act silly

11. Legume named after a city

13. Early trial presentation

15. Cut into glass

17. King's address

19. Big shade trees

20. Bathroom fixture

Answers on page 177.

WHATNOTS

ACROSS

1. Bridge's length
3. Shelter offerings
9. Lack of guile
10. Boot out
11. Total amazingness
13. Prairie howler
15. Menlo Park mastermind
17. "No rush at all"
20. "The Lion King" king
21. Green gem
22. Is behind
23. Very shrewd

DOWN

1. Big film festival name
2. Whisper to the audience
4. Brunch dish
5. Reception for a politician or celebrity
6. Cousins of llamas
7. Enticing store sign
8. "Shape up!"
12. How some medicines should be taken
14. "Definitely, dude!"
16. Clear and convincing
18. Gem State
19. Computer buyer

Answers on page 177.

ACROSS

1. Molar, maybe
7. Discharged
8. "Aha!"
10. Get out of one's chair
11. Bent the elbow
12. Come to visit
14. Pretty soon
17. Came to a halt
19. Had an impact
21. Shakespeare's Falstaff
22. Film legend Garbo
23. Intuitive feeling

DOWN

1. Sources of juice?
2. Begin a voyage
3. Prayer beginning
4. Like psychedelic music
5. Ad nauseam
6. "Laughing" beast
9. Be a lulu
13. Geezer
15. Burglarized
16. Luck of the draw
18. Head covering
20. Prepare to advance on a fly

Answers on page 177.

IN PHOTO AND PRINT

ACROSS

5. Happen as expected

7. Coastal breeze

8. Before you know it

9. Feel certain

10. It's for wide-angle shots

12. Behind-the-scenes author

14. Lodge group

15. "Green Acres" costar

17. At a cruise stop

18. "You're right after all"

DOWN

1. Built from

2. Cunning

3. Legs and thighs

4. Action figures with dog tags

6. Inability to dance

7. Eye and ear

11. Where to buy footwear

12. Try for a Hail Mary pass

13. Flat mate

16. What you can take from me

Answers on page 178.

TO-DO LIST

ACROSS

1. Canine line?
4. All the same
8. Used influence
10. Bite-sized Asian food
11. Generally speaking
12. Currently
16. Area far from port
18. "Gulliver's Travels" brute
20. Washes plates and such
21. Fake blazer
22. Implement that must be wrung

DOWN

1. Way around the city
2. Beguiling tricks
3. 5,280 feet
5. Earth, in some sci-fi
6. Emotional inhibitions
7. Academic hanger
9. Cold War competition
12. Program with an anchor
13. "Glad I could help!"
14. Show off on a skateboard, e.g.
15. An even chance
17. Altercation
19. "How boring!"

Answers on page 178.

X MARKS THE SPOT

ACROSS

1. Release
5. Camera lens setting
8. Goes up and down
9. Final consumer
10. Athlete's thirst quencher
11. Become ragged
13. Trade center
16. "Confess!"
17. Elicit
20. Carrier making short hops
21. All together, in music
22. Automotive dud
23. Barely beat

DOWN

1. Birds do it
2. "Have a bite!"
3. Picket line phrase
4. Military practice
5. Become harder to see
6. Dress rehearsal
7. Bright and bouncy
12. Frustrating series of calls
14. Crude container
15. Accept blame quietly
16. Batting game for kids
18. "A Tale ___ Cities"
19. Advise of danger

Answers on page 178.

ACROSS

6. Unrestricted military conflict

8. Sow's opposite

9. Operation Overlord event

10. "For example?"

12. Singing genre of the '50s

13. "Beats me"

15. By agreed order

16. Scott Joplin's jazz

18. Bouquet holder

19. Salon coloring target

DOWN

1. Fail in business

2. Playground set

3. Gofer task

4. A little insight?

5. Entrance on a farm

7. Extreme laissez-faire

11. Doing well on the links

14. Circular seals

15. "The ___ Cometh"

17. Colorful eye part

Answers on page 178.

BUCKETS OF B'S

ACROSS

1. Sports car feature
7. Bathday cake
8. Acquired family member
9. Affair of honor
10. Become lenient
13. "Act your age!"
15. Odd fellow
17. Should it be that
18. Bridge player's "I pass"
22. "If it only could be"
23. Some things to mind
24. Make an error

DOWN

1. Boat that's towed
2. Camp food
3. Have on the payroll
4. Jump past
5. Dream team pick
6. Boars' mates
7. Disreputable sort
11. Marksman
12. "Haven't heard a thing"
14. About 2.2 pounds
16. "No sweat!"
19. Sing across the Alps
20. Like Bill Hickok
21. Bangalore bigwig

Answers on page 179.

INTELLIGENCE AND KNOWLEDGE

ACROSS

6. "Don't mumble!"

8. Be a comedian

9. Barely discernible

10. "Remain where you are"

11. Raymond in "Rain Man," say

14. Editor's assistant

17. Possible weapon in a bar fight

18. Diet-friendly, informally

19. "Lemon Tree" singer Lopez

20. Loop in one's pocket

DOWN

1. Loud lakeside rental

2. Pretty good

3. Child's game

4. Accept eagerly

5. In on, like a cool cat

6. Considered it proper

7. Seller of stamps and such

12. Conveyer of dip

13. AI computer language

14. Get there by walking

15. Begin to take effect

16. Words of likelihood

18. Produces eggs

Answers on page 179.

FOOD AND DRINK

ACROSS

1. Watches one's mouth?
5. Spit out
8. A crankshaft drives it
9. Clarifying exchange
10. Difficult situations
12. "Not so fast!"
14. Command to relax
16. Prohibitionists' target
19. Mo of Arizona politics
20. Be unfaithful to
21. "For Pete's ___!"
22. Candlelit spot, perhaps

DOWN

1. Brit's elevator
2. Beverage in a big bowl
3. Shocking fish
4. Duplication marks
6. Box opener of myth
7. "How you doin'?"
9. Single-beat symbol, often
11. Decathlon events in a circle
13. Recline
15. "Have a good day!" reply
17. American Indian corn
18. Shed a tear

Answers on page 179.

CROSSWORD AT CAPACITY

ACROSS

1. Implied subtly
7. Journalist
8. "Enter the Dragon" star Bruce
9. Stage of grief
10. HS lab class
11. Motif
13. University study group
15. Official with a pistol
17. "Have a great time!"
21. Chicken morsel
22. Mr. Darcy's creator
23. Beauty salon goop
24. Downloadable sound
25. Castle features

DOWN

1. Football headgear
2. Cleopatra's ___
3. Exhaust, as strength
4. Competed in a bee
5. Small portion
6. Home of the Red Cross
12. Home buyer's loan
14. Beirut's country
16. Material for pub quizzes
18. Mowgli's habitat
19. Gives the right-of-way
20. A plus

Answers on page 179.

FIGURATIVE PHRASES

ACROSS

5. Act like a couch potato

7. Disappointing disparity

8. Anticrime boss

9. Have insomnia

10. Short distance

12. Poor people

14. Went away

16. Arsenal items

17. Expression of disapproval

18. Ending unhappily

DOWN

1. Appropriates

2. Discordant tone

3. "Enterprise" personnel

4. Former NBC anchor Tom

6. Discussed

7. Sweat due to pressure

11. Shields, tear gas, etc.

12. Began a golf game

13. Brought off the bench

15. "Black Swan" attire

Answers on page 180.

KEEPING QUIET

ACROSS

7. Cheer for

8. Emphatic refusal

9. Narc squad member, e.g.

11. Record an exit

13. Computer peripheral, e.g.

14. Eminem's mentor

15. Elects, as a politician

17. Hush-hush treatment

20. Very long cold snap

21. " You ___!" ("Sure!")

DOWN

1. Class clowns, e.g.

2. "Yipes!"

3. Checkerboard comment

4. Outstanding

5. Numbers of letters

6. Suppress, as emotions

10. Scale ranges

12. Bestowed by the deity

13. Symbol on a violist's sheet music

14. Enter headlong

16. Speak against

18. Slavic girl's name

19. Apply acid artistically

Answers on page 180.

SINK AND A DRINK

ACROSS

1. Spicy condiment
5. Aberdeen resident
8. Successful hitter's asset
9. Gasket type
10. Area in London or New York
11. Clue weapon
13. Sink
15. Gene Roddenberry series
17. Bounce across water
20. Bright planet
21. "Am I early?"
22. Never again, in slang
23. Abrupt ending

DOWN

1. Euphoric feelings
2. Kind of foul, in basketball
3. Bowled over
4. Peppermint liqueur
6. "Five-alarm" dish
7. Pair of wrestlers
9. Fewer than 100 shares
12. Current condition
13. Appliance with a pilot
14. Go on a date with
16. Texas ___ University
18. Arrange in a bun, e.g.
19. C, in bathrooms

Answers on page 180.

FAMILIAR PHRASES

ACROSS

1. When day breaks
4. Andy Warhol genre
8. Seek, as an office
9. Curly or Larry
11. People you recognize
12. Emotional identification
17. Expressed indirectly
18. A bit much
19. Cheated off a test, maybe
20. Irregular, as fog
21. Churchill gestures

DOWN

1. Floating aimlessly
2. Eager beaver
3. Elephant ancestor
5. No longer in danger
6. Immediately
7. Itsy-bitsy
10. Garfield's favorite dish
13. Circus tent
14. Do an usher's work
15. "For ___ out loud!"
16. Backs of hits

Answers on page 180.

ABC, APPLE, BALL, CRAB

ACROSS

7. Iffy issue

8. "The Daily Show" host Trevor

9. Compete on Halloween

10. Ad come-on, redundantly

13. Back up, as files

14. Cabinet drawer opener

16. Many a pop tune

18. Handle responsibility, so to speak

21. Battery unit

22. Entertainment for night owls

DOWN

1. Be a grouch

2. "Ciao for now!"

3. 2012 Affleck film

4. Semitic congratulations

5. Built without a contract

6. Flag on a coat

11. Goes bananas

12. Pointless chatter

15. Mechanical way to learn

17. Few and far between

19. Beanery sign

20. Appear imminent

Answers on page 181.

CLUE STEW

ACROSS

1. Small power source
6. What to do after a shampoo
7. Sat for a photo
9. Go unhurriedly
10. Like some lunch orders
11. Accompany
13. Fast food burger
16. Capital of New Mexico
18. "Wheel of Fortune" buy
20. "Hound Dog" singer
21. Casino VIP
22. Places to pull off the highway

DOWN

1. Enola Gay payload
2. Creditor's loss
3. Holder of balls and dolls
4. American in Paris, e.g.
5. "Of course, dear lady"
6. Noble act
8. "Work beckons!"
12. Persuaded
14. Kind of fertilization
15. Dangles a carrot before
17. Altar recesses
19. Cabin location

Answers on page 181.

AIR AND SPACE

ACROSS

5. Fruity cookie

7. Cups and saucers

9. "Battlestar Galactica" and such

10. Do a spit take, e.g.

11. Term of endearment

13. Completely rational

15. Adoring Biblical trio

17. Takes the plunge

19. Afraid to fire

20. Type of date on food packaging

DOWN

1. Closes, as a windbreaker

2. Nonworking hours

3. Brand of swabs

4. Handles the details of

6. Say what you saw in court

8. Where people get off of planes

12. Fried egg option

14. Eases off

16. "Great" fictional character

18. "Empire" actor Diggs

Answers on page 181.

LOTS OF B'S

ACROSS

1. Picnic drink holder

6. Fancy-schmancy

8. Film with a chariot race

9. Amusingly twisted

10. City of David

11. A bit bawdy

12. Tear dabber

14. Little traveled way

15. Mild stimulant from a palm tree

17. Exploded, with "up"

18. Business owner's goal

19. Having posted bond

20. Annoying kid

21. Announcement medium

DOWN

2. Mistake by the staff

3. "Hallelujah" Leonard

4. Place for a stud

5. Artful Dodger, for one

6. Chance for a shot

7. Vessel intended for combat

13. Stay in shape

14. Ballpark aides

16. Still asleep

17. How some students get to school

Answers on page 181.

IN THE WILD

ACROSS

4. Cross the threshold
5. "Amen!"
7. Former incarnation
9. Calcium source
10. Lions and tigers and bears
13. Cause trouble
15. Leave at the altar
16. Barking wanderer
18. Monk habitats
19. Clove hitch, for example

DOWN

1. Gold from the Magi, e.g.
2. Mail from a sweetheart
3. "You're blocking the view!"
4. Egg carton rating
6. Absorbent powder
8. "No way, Jose!"
11. Lab vessel
12. Gracefully step down
14. "Me, me, me" sort
17. Abrupt pull

Answers on page 182.

MERRY MEDLEY

ACROSS

1. Freight sent by plane

5. "Dinner's ready" sound

8. Europe, Asia and Africa

9. Bourbon Street side

11. Exhale with relief

14. Far and wide

15. Toy pistol

17. Blue footwear for Elvis

20. "Dream on!"

21. Clean with a broom

22. The Knickerbockers song about mendacity

23. "That's life!"

DOWN

1. A bad way to run

2. Ill-mannered

3. Financially viable

4. Cut to a roving reporter

6. Nuclear research city

7. Greet effusively

10. At-ease position for soldiers

12. Basic grading system

13. Something for nothing

16. "Tommy" band

18. Big name in clowning

19. Mayberry cell dweller

Answers on page 182.

AN OCULAR PUZZLE

ACROSS

7. "As we speak…"

9. Athlete's best effort

10. Lovely to look on

11. "S.N.L." alum Cheri

13. Offs, gangsterstyle

16. "Deal with it!"

17. Artillery discharge

18. They help you see

21. Cry of despair

22. Cheer on

DOWN

1. "OK, I'm starting now…"

2. A minor and others

3. Quick as a wink

4. Bake sale item

5. Raggedy Ann, for one

6. Own (up)

8. Appliance needed for a hot bath

12. Delighting in

14. Greyhound station, e.g.

15. Suit bottom

18. Armed forces VIP

19. "Beg your pardon…"

20. Umpire's call

Answers on page 182.

TAKE A CHANCE

ACROSS

7. California racetrack

8. Comes up

9. Try something out

10. Queens stadium name

12. Loyal politician

14. Prime minister of Queen Victoria's reign

16. Emma Stone's "___ Land"

17. Last-ditch play

20. Exit the system

21. Atlantic archipelago

DOWN

1. Arctic Sea floater

2. Cheap flick

3. Peach cobbler, for example

4. "Til next time!"

5. "A ___ Fortress Is Our God"

6. Where steins are raised

11. Crow's-nest cry

13. Something to save for

15. Deodorant on a ball

16. Apply pressure to

18. Volvo or VW

19. Get angrier and angrier

Answers on page 182.

FROM FACE TO FEET

ACROSS

1. Large depression for water
5. Bouillon bits
8. "Goodbye, Pierre"
9. Male protagonist
10. Salon employee
12. Benedictine head
14. Aisle worker
16. They come on when you stop
19. Generic images
20. "Add to cart" business
21. Unifying idea
22. Creator of the Grinch

DOWN

1. Goof off
2. Richards of the Stones
3. Like someone tired of talking
4. Collection of abridged works
5. Wait
6. Standout in a small pond
7. Con artists
11. Feline with a mottled coat
13. Bad way to get beat
15. Left at the altar
17. Noted performing whale
18. "Sound of Music" setting

Answers on page 183.

CLUE ACCUMULATION

ACROSS

7. All-purpose fix-it roll

8. "Hey, sailor!"

9. Feeling happy

10. Handy carryall

12. Emotion-hiding sort

14. Coral ridges

16. Robotic space probe

19. Less than a warm welcome

21. "High" places for pirates

22. Guide to getting around a mall

DOWN

1. Change directions

2. Took long steps

3. "Mister" who might help you sleep

4. A metronome marks it

5. Pirate's bird

6. Gondolier's offering

11. Egg quantity, often

13. Garrison Keillor's Lake

15. Down-home; unstudied and rustic

17. Duds

18. Blue-and-white pottery

20. A Washington office shape

Answers on page 183.

WRITTEN AND SPOKEN

ACROSS

7. Inbox clutter

8. "Let's do this thing!"

9. Type of radio enthusiast

10. Be extremely frugal

12. "It was a dark and ___ night..."

14. Develop

16. Hunting lures

17. Parting words

20. Sonnet source

21. "Stop," for one

DOWN

1. Overdo the sentiment

2. Dieter's drink

3. Intensify

4. Dust jacket comments

5. Droop in the heat

6. Game with sets and runs

11. Slow cooker

13. Obviously

15. Gripping tool

16. Perform perfectly

18. Start of a piercing rebuke?

19. Above the strike zone

Answers on page 183.

CURIOUS CROSSWORD

ACROSS

5. Nursery rhyme shepherdess

7. Variety show of "Kornfield Kounty"

8. Start to a breakup letter

9. A neighbor of Thailand

10. Easy as ABC

12. "Be right there"

14. Beyonce in "Cadillac Records"

15. Youngsters

17. Hold back

18. Digestive aid

DOWN

1. Chinese noodle dish

2. Anjou or Bosc

3. In the money

4. Exit door

6. Spendthrift in a parable

7. Battlefield "pineapple"

11. Get rid of

12. Elite flying group

13. "The Sound of Music" song

16. Averse to work

Answers on page 183.

A PHRASE AND A SONG

ACROSS

1. "Piece of cake!"
5. Hard-sell phrase
8. "Got it, dude"
9. Liturgical assistant
10. Small looking glass
12. Kept waiting, with "along"
14. Third largest ocean
15. Jailed, or like a mixologist
18. One that runs through town
19. At hand
20. "Admit it!"
21. "Buy one get one free" offer

DOWN

2. Seasoned seamen
3. Like a hard-liner
4. Getting off, in court
5. In the early hours, to Eric Clapton
6. Show embarrassment
7. "My bad!"
11. Legitimate target
13. Frees from the ropes
16. Earl Scruggs' instrument
17. Shake the confidence of

Answers on page 184.

DECISIONS AND QUESTIONS

ACROSS

1. Decide by chance
8. NYC landmark
9. Legendary lady killer
10. Polite response to "Thank you"
11. "E.R." actor La Salle
13. Uncle Sam's lid
15. "Beat it!"
17. Confiscated auto
18. Last-minute loss of nerve
21. Some live-in emigres
22. "The Jetsons" dog
23. One way to seal a deal

DOWN

1. Breakfast loaf
2. Highly skilled
3. Golf hazard
4. Fill full of holes
5. Blink of an eye
6. ___ Rico
7. Offer to clarify further
12. Money in hand
14. Infield flies
16. Has some success
19. Chow down at home
20 Genie's grant

Answers on page 184.

STORIES AND MUSIC

ACROSS

1. Cowardly type
8. #1 Beatles hit of 1970
9. "___ Andronicus"
11. Time between birthdays
12. Out of the woods
14. "The Ransom of Red Chief" writer
15. Draws a bead on
18. Wordless comic bit
20. Crunchy Mexican food
22. City in Dade County
23. Mother lode
24. "Nice and slow"

DOWN

2. Dirt-cheap
3. Peanuts expletive
4. Made use of
5. Honeybunch
6. Academic aide
7. Pretend to be asleep
10. Sugar craving
13. Candidates not on ballots
16. Official language of Kenya
17. Barked like a peke
19. Blow a fuse
21. Dark alter ego

Answers on page 184.

COLLECTIBLES AND PRECIOUS THINGS

ACROSS

1. According to schedule
4. Camera settings
8. Los Angeles district
9. Endured
10. Children's toy on tracks
12. "Au contraire!"
17. Add-on to a bill
18. Enter via keyboard
19. Burning up
20. 1960s protests
21. On top of that

DOWN

1. Like a play without intermission
2. Add at the last moment
3. Perfect shape, to a collector
5. Whispered words into a lovers' ears
6. Father or husband
7. Lying on one's back
11. Belly bump
13. If nothing changes
14. "Change the subject already!"
15. Carbon dioxide, as a solid
16. Breakfast bowl filler

Answers on page 184.

TOOLS AND GEMS

ACROSS

1. Freak out
6. Fill the suitcase
8. Big blowout
9. Remove the soap from
10. Arm of the Atlantic
11. Tiniest bit
12. U-shaped part of a road
14. Well-seasoned
15. Billiards maneuver
17. David Copperfield offering
18. Comply with
19. "Modern Family" dad
20. Meryl/Roseanne movie

DOWN

2. Playground comeback
3. Power tool for making holes
4. Gets comfortable
5. Sykes of standup
6. Diamond, for one
7. Have faith in
12. "Baloney!"
13. "No, No" girl of Broadway
15. Button material
16. "Liar Liar" actress Cheri

Answers on page 185.

A BIT OF WORDPLAY

ACROSS

1. "Star Wars" pilot
5. Bus station
8. Musical staff symbol
9. Sirius (or Lassie?)
10. Extremely simple
13. Became waterless
14. Christie of whodunits
17. Get suspicious
21. Get some air
22. End of the Pacific war
23. Big name in copiers
24. Destroyers, in Navy lingo

DOWN

1. Bigger than big
2. "Antony and Cleopatra" river
3. 2019, 2021, or 2023, with respect to elections
4. Somewhat passé
5. Fixed belief
6. Miniature golf, informally
7. Like some light bulbs
11. Media section
12. Canal site
15. Exact revenge
16. High-priority
18. House paint ingredient
19. "Aha moment" cause
20. "Y" facilities

Answers on page 185.

TUNEFUL PHRASES

ACROSS

5. Toddler's owie

7. Mass arrival

9. Elevator tunes, e.g.

10. Baked custard

11. Like some bridges

13. Game is protected here

15. Insurer's calculation

17. Related things, slangily

19. Didn't stop

20. "The Bourne Identity" author Robert

DOWN

1. Diet food ad phrase

2. Eager beaver

3. Al dente

4. Brunch pie

6. Cool, fruity dessert

8. Skip past, as commercials

12. Order during an MRI

14. Gadded about

16. Give the onceover

18. Driver's protest

Answers on page 185.

TEST YOUR KNOWLEDGE

ACROSS

7. Barely managed

8. Town of a man with seven wives

9. Vein or artery

10. A few cross words

12. How good friends may walk

14. Unfortunate turn of events

16. Wearisome voyage

17. Light and dark ice cream flavor

20. Calendar girls, e.g.

21. "Enough already!"

DOWN

1. Shakespeare's foot

2. Make larger, at the tailor's shop

3. Commendable reputation

4. Wight or Man

5. Makes an unwanted pass at

6. "Be my guest!"

11. Observe the rules

13. Captain Picard's catchphrase

15. Source of mattress misery

16. Alpha male

18. "Piece of cake!"

19. Wicked stuff

Answers on page 185.

BEST TIME FOR A PARTY

ACROSS

1. One, of, the, errors, here
8. Groom's last hurrah
9. Accepted eagerly
10. First part of a process
11. Hemingway or Tubb
13. Some plasterwork
17. Circulatory conduit
19. Billiard ball bounce
20. Inferred okay
21. Very soon

DOWN

1. Cost of a taxi
2. Personified detergent
3. Lots, as of trouble
4. Build a fire under
5. Safety restraint
6. Title villain of a James Bond flick
7. What Orpheus strummed
12. Infatuated with
14. Desert procession
15. Electrician's rule
16. "Enough already!"
17. A bit pretentious
18. The Indy 500 drivers, for one
19. Circular storage medium

Answers on page 186.

BIRDS AND FLOWERS

ACROSS

1. Symbols of America
7. "To sum up..."
8. Tony or Obie
10. First light
13. Fried chicken choice
14. Alluring beachwear
17. Indignant reply
21. Opera house, with "la"
22. Get to the bottom of
23. Comfortable situation

DOWN

1. Control tower image
2. Filled with greenery
3. Display of self-importance
4. Blow a gasket
5. A sister of Calliope
6. Boo-boo protector
9. Wry humor
11. Dirty looks
12. First garment material
15. By mistake
16. Cares for
18. Bowled over
19. Trunk growth
20. Singer Redding

Answers on page 186.

Q MARKS THE SPOT

ACROSS

1. White orb with no number
5. Artist's theme
8. Singer LaBelle
9. Marshmallow sandwich
10. Hard labor spot
11. Homeless child
13. New Orleans district
15. Cafe au ___
17. Captain Hook's foe
20. "Imagine that!"
21. One score after deuce
22. "Over There" soldiers
23. Bureaucratic nonsense

DOWN

1. Manages somehow
2. Getty of "The Golden Girls"
3. More than one can handle
4. Tool for making tart fruit juice
5. Kitty's comment
6. Aggressive sort
7. Sympathize with
12. King, queen or jack
13. One left holding the bag
14. Dessert pudding
16. Explanatory intro
18. "Find somebody else!"
19. In this way

Answers on page 186.

VALENTINE'S DAY

ACROSS

7. Cart away

9. 18, generally

10. Godiva choice

11. Clever people

12. Attack from above

15. Mike, to Archie Bunker

16. Look at

19. How many fall in love

21. Reformer Ralph

22. Way up the slope

DOWN

1. Follow covertly

2. Way to prepare potatoes

3. Express, as an opinion

4. Become a sailor

5. Gulf of California peninsula

6. Amp effect

8. Sunshine State vacation area

13. Dressing component

14. Part of the team

15. Egyptian tourist attraction

17. Aware of

18. Arab chief

20. Nurse's assistant

Answers on page 186.

A VACATION FROM CLEANING

ACROSS

7. Ancient Chinese text

8. Add water to

9. It really sucks

11. Compare the costs of

13. Have too much sun, perhaps

15. All shook up

17. Absolutely detest

18. Common policy on vacation time

20. Stop, as a leak

21. Former justice Antonin

DOWN

1. Venom source

2. All the rage

3. Like harmonious bands

4. Musical deficiency

5. Directly up, on a map

6. Become tattered

10. French wine region

12. Where to nip it

14. Pub hurlers

16. Kind of test

17. Without further ado

18. Ballpark figures

19. Aquatic zappers

Answers on page 187.

FUN AND GAMES

ACROSS

1. Boxer's weak spot
5. Belt hole makers
8. Pronoun of the queen
9. Art gallery
10. Carried, as a gun
11. Get a sense of
12. "Big Easy" festival
15. Headlight setting
16. Start of a series
18. Water threesome
19. Nobody at all
20. Kind of rock music
21. Intimidate

DOWN

1. Do the twist
2. At this point
3. Spinach, lettuce, etc.
4. Boss in a red suit
6. Small parts
7. Performed a ballad for
9. Example of dirty politics
12. Decimate, as an army
13. "Li'l Abner" cartoonist
14. Achieve success
17. 8x10, for one

Answers on page 187.

FIGURATIVE PLACES

ACROSS

1. Be a guest of
8. Veteran sailors
9. Hired muscle
10. "Y.M.C.A." singers
11. Accept a proposal
13. Regained consciousness
17. Easy task
20. "Not gonna do it!"
21. Things may disappear here
22. Big dog

DOWN

1. Compared with
2. Head and shoulders cover
3. "Missed your chance!"
4. Like a good drill team
5. "I'll take a card"
6. Kid's dirty "dessert"
7. "Duly noted"
12. Brick road color
14. Endured humiliation
15. Symbol of might
16. Venus de Milo, for one
17. Prodigy, in slang
18. Suitcase label
19. Arabian gulf

Answers on page 187.

KNOWLEDGE IS POWER

ACROSS

1. Fizzy drink with flavored syrup
6. Like press-on fingernails
8. Gov't investments
9. Refused
10. "Could be worse"
11. Currently plentiful
12. Excited like Miss Piggy?
16. 2006 movie of Helen Mirren
18. Dock area
19. Before it's too late
20. One and all, among guys
21. Avian bill
22. Flavor detector

DOWN

2. Seek revenge against
3. Hurt deeply
4. Subsequent
5. Covers up
6. On the level
7. More or less
13. Fires up
14. Loose coins
15. Coleridge setting
17. Apply with intensity

Answers on page 187.

AROUND THE WORLD

ACROSS

1. Vatican sentinel
7. Andean wool source
8. Feels at home
10. Elongated key
11. Home of Baylor University
13. Admission of guilt
15. Big game caravan
17. Gently urge
18. Polite prevarication
21. Be dressed in
22. ___ Domingo
23. Behave yourself

DOWN

1. Car dealer's spiel, e.g.
2. Ivanka's mom
3. Place of turmoil
4. Old Glory, briefly
5. Big cracker brand
6. Noisy summer bug
9. House trailer
12. Tacky quality
14. After a fashion
16. "What's there to lose?"
19. Hawaiian island or a veranda
20. Cancun coin

Answers on page 188.

FILL IN THE PHRASE

ACROSS

1. Freak out
6. Pushes, as a pedal
7. Deep sadness
9. German WWII sub
10. No longer current
11. Goldberg of "Sister Act"
13. See the light
16. How close races are won
18. Fish and rice rolls
20. Case for Mulder
21. Full speed
22. What many older parents face

DOWN

1. Artist El ___
2. Dot on a transit map
3. Corporal or sergeant
4. Dark hours
5. One stuck in the snow
6. Intercom speaker
8. Contractual details
12. Dramatic way to stop
14. Like a trained athlete
15. Insect enemy of citrus
17. A point ahead
19. "Get moving!"

Answers on page 188.

TANGLED UP

ACROSS

1. Be honest with yourself
4. Classified item
8. "Don't blame somebody else!"
10. Flat piece of microfilm
11. Information requests
12. Say when enough is enough
16. Knesset member
18. Former columnist Hopper
19. "Popeye" episode, for example
20. Tries to mislead
21. Crossed the threshold

DOWN

1. Leave on a jet plane, e.g.
2. Worship event
3. Check for quality
5. "What's it all about?" guy
6. Evert
7. Can't stomach
9. Mighty fine
13. At the last minute, say
14. Greeting with a drawl
15. Egg container
17. Put on a pedestal

Answers on page 188.

PATCHWORK

ACROSS

1. Hitchhike
6. Baby bed
8. Exactly like this
9. Computer bug
10. Sheet music symbol
11. Entered formally
12. Sandwich bread choices
14. "Well done!"
16. "At Last" singer James
18. "I'd almost forgotten..."
19. Big part of an order
20. Bowls over
21. Way beyond the booths

DOWN

2. Garden-variety
3. Random good deed, perhaps
4. "Speaking personally..."
5. All fired up
6. Penny saver, at times
7. Driver's license and such
12. Expertise
13. Bad bargain
15. Cymbals with a foot pedal
17. '70s courtroom drama

Answers on page 188.

ON THE SCREEN OR IN NATURE

ACROSS

7. Coleslaw, often
8. Hopped a plane
9. Goldie Hawn flick or desert bloom
10. AARP member
12. "Forget about it!"
14. Journalist's basics
16. Bowling alley worker, once
17. Young people's drama of old
20. "___ me up, Scotty!"
21. Black gold

DOWN

1. "Wassup!"
2. Simple word processing format
3. California coastal region
4. Jill of "The Love Boat"
5. Hardly any
6. In the old days
11. Villain's exploit
13. Nautical danger
15. Give some lip to
16. Turn down
18. Sonogram area
19. Give off

Answers on page 189.

RAGBAG

ACROSS

1. Positive behaviors

7. One way to travel

8. George Washington, for one

9. "You agree?"

10. "...but I might be wrong"

11. Bake-shop sweet

13. Duel option

16. Aired out

18. Reach the sum of

20. Second phase

21. Poker raise, at times

22. Malfunctioning

DOWN

1. Monthly utility item

2. Arkansas range

3. Question for a brown cow

4. Including everything

5. "Country club" in NYC

6. Spot for Tennessee Williams' cat

7. Place for a stick

12. On the carpet

14. Classroom surprise

15. Buy, as a politician

17. Cause winter isolation

19. Emirate on the Persian Gulf

Answers on page 189.

FRESH BATCH

ACROSS

1. Acknowledge royalty
5. Big swallow
8. "Don't sweat it!"
9. Minimal amount
11. State-of-the-art
13. "The Handmaid's Tale" author
14. Spoke fluent bumblebee?
17. Diamond topper
20. "Uncle!"
21. Not a single soul
22. "The Dragons of ___"
23. Private place for paramours

DOWN

1. Rub out
2. Goes ballistic
3. Be mischievous
4. Animal in an exercise wheel
6. Bring to bear
7. Prepare
10. Portage vessel
12. Soldier's spouse, sometimes
15. Numbers on letters
16. Rookie's mentor
18. Grab hold of
19. "B there in 5," e.g.

Answers on page 189.

PHRASE ASSORTMENT

ACROSS

1. Dude ranch visitor

7. Arm of the Atlantic

8. Tease relentlessly

9. Inner circle member

10. Not quite with it

11. Basketball strategy

14. Nonstandard auto feature

16. Have no doubt

18. Apple or mountain

19. Personification of America

20. Classic Christmas carol

DOWN

1. Atoll material

2. Anti-nuke action

3. Full of back talk

4. Right away

5. "M*A*S*H" setting

6. House of Lancaster emblem

11. Homemade weapons

12. Ladies' man

13. Savings for later in life

15. "Consider it done!"

16. Breakfast meat

17. Tribute with good-natured ribbing

Answers on page 189.

FANTASTIC PHRASES

ACROSS

1. Don't give up
6. "Arizona" Memorial site
8. Settle in for the long haul
9. "The golden years"
10. Big Apple museum, for short
11. Actor's makeup
14. "For shame!"
16. Earl Grey holder
18. "Listen up!"
19. Each, in pricing
20. Place for a bar

DOWN

2. Boot out
3. "Cutie pie" or "sweetie"
4. Collector's stash
5. Shirt without sleeves
6. Atmospheric layer
7. Difficult spot
11. Old street fixture
12. Caribbean destination
13. Behind the eight ball
15. "Lady and the ___"
16. "Delta Dawn" singer Tucker
17. Sisters of parents

Answers on page 190.

CLASSIC CROSSWORD

ACROSS

1. Board game accessory
6. Deli orders
8. Ascend
9. "On the house"
10. Plan, as an itinerary
11. Like a live ball
12. "Hang on..."
15. Some charity tourneys
17. Minuteman's weapon
19. Stinging crawlers
20. '80s rock group
21. Gets along in years
22. Stubbornly resists defeat

DOWN

2. Climate change
3. Blood bank's universal donor
4. Herbal brew
5. Lizzie Borden portrayer Christina
6. Do a hair salon job
7. Artie Shaw, for example
13. Out of order
14. All together
16. Assembly of church leaders
18. Lawn mower's path

Answers on page 190.

ODDS AND ENDS

ACROSS

6. Campus cadet's org.

7. To reciprocate

9. Player near the shortstop

10. For a while

11. Apply hastily

13. Motto of the brave

15. Hired guns

16. Unseen observer

18. Unaided sight

19. Attend, as a school

DOWN

1. Early James Bond foe

2. Hidden advantage

3. Solomon specialty

4. Bach may be played on them

5. Delivery from a diva

8. Eventual vindication

12. Serving until midnight, say

14. Way past ripe

15. Gave ear to

17. Problem for a waterbed or for Watergate

Answers on page 190.

MIX IT UP

ACROSS

2. Puts up with

6. Antacid ingredient

8. Like a tree-lined street

9. Review hastily

10. Banquet snack

13. Going ahead of the group

14. Dining quickly

19. Blue ___ Cult

20. Plea to Lassie

21. Made use of

22. Robin Hood's gang

23. Had a chat

DOWN

1. Take close aim

2. Cut in two

3. Wildly enthusiastic

4. Familiar saying

5. Australian metropolis

6. Small arms technique

7. Spend more than you have

11. It "sweeps clean"

12. Roman temple

14. Proficient in

15. In addition

16. Change into

17. Got the creases out

18. Croix de ___ (French medal)

Answers on page 190.

POTPOURRI

ACROSS

1. Rooks on a chessboard
5. Inactive, as gases
8. Mosey along
9. "Jaws" town
10. New mother's hangout
12. Gobs
14. Garden pavilion
16. ID for an investment
19. Jason jilted her
20. Revolving fishing lure
21. Turn aside, as a gaze
22. Ice cream alternative

DOWN

1. Volume of precedents
2. Fledgling pigeon
3. Brunch, essentially
4. Turin relic
5. Thing you may be dared to cross
6. Connoisseur of fine dining
7. Blocks, trains, tops, etc.
11. Chew out
13. Waste away
15. Light refractors
17. Country inn, briefly
18. "Harry Potter" actress Watson

Answers on page 191.

FLOTSAM AND JETSAM

ACROSS

7. Fib

8. "I'm sure I can think of something…"

9. Diplomat's asset

10. Snoop Dogg or Ice-T

12. Naan or pumpernickel

14. Canoe bark

16. Films before "talkies"

19. Chomp down on

20. Astronomers study it

22. Minimal work-groups

DOWN

1. DNA element

2. Camel relatives

3. Like a so-so movie rating

4. Arm wrestler's pride

5. Take under one's wing

6. Infographic with wedges

11. Guy full of excuses

13. Cannons or VIPs

15. Bayou cuisine

17. Total

18. Clove hitch and granny

21. Bird on a New Zealand dollar

Answers on page 191.

CORNUCOPIA

ACROSS

1. Ski-slope transport
5. Angry crowd
7. Like Simba or Elsa
8. Cattle country
9. Goes into in detail
13. Alaskan native
14. Overstep a boundary
17. Chinos color
18. Clownfish's home
19. Card that may be high or low
20. Readily understood

DOWN

1. Dead-end road
2. Bikini, notably
3. It's used in laying down a track
4. Put more pressure (on)
5. Asian rainy season
6. Butcher-shop buy
10. Happening
11. "Ditto!"
12. Artillery onslaught
15. Apples you listen to
16. Big name in do-it-yourself furniture

Answers on page 191.

PANOPLY

ACROSS

7. Getty or Guggenheim
8. Connive
9. Geisha belts
10. Word for word
11. Uses an awl
13. Cruel smile
15. Compete in a roller derby
17. Song for baby
20. Educator's job
21. "Yeah, yeah"
22. Type of pine or grain
23. Plane's odometerlike device

DOWN

1. Bombay, today
2. Animated toon frames
3. Second-rate flicks
4. Seize by force
5. Shell fragments
6. Ballpark official
12. Good news for borrowers
14. Thief who breaks in
16. Yiddish whine
18. Yogi Bear's sidekick
19. Easy to lift
21. Brute of folklore

Answers on page 191.

KNICKKNACKS

ACROSS

1. Bob Dylan's specialty
6. 3, 4 or 5 on a golf course
8. Ottawa's province
9. Feet in a meter
10. Seesaw
12. Chips and salsa treat
14. "Mutiny on the Bounty" island
16. Resources for a specific purpose
19. Pocatello's state
20. Abdomen
21. Accelerator pedal
22. "C'mon, let's go!"

DOWN

1. Cake topping
2. Bat maker's machine
3. Blackbird collective
4. Like a closely-shaven cheek
5. "Pale Rider" star
6. City buried by Vesuvius eruption
7. Garden beauty
11. Place for merlots and pinots
13. Pirate's sword
15. Candy heart command
17. Adjust to change
18. Checkmate target

Answers on page 192.

JUMBLE

ACROSS

1. Orator's pedestal
5. "Boring!"
8. Geico's mascot
9. Deadening
10. "Do unto others..." maxim
11. Rowdy disorder
12. Emergency situation
15. Nit-picking
18. Just for fun
19. Decree from the king
20. "My Big Fat ___ Wedding"
21. "A thousand pardons!"

DOWN

1. Impressive spectacle
2. Robin Hood's skill
3. Go ballistic
4. "Stately pleasuredome" site
5. Contortionists
6. 17-syllable poem
7. Fridge stickers
11. Chinese tile game
13. Less bland
14. Some cereals
16. Dazzled
17. Showing spunk

Answers on page 192.

DOODADS

ACROSS

1. Layered pasta dish
5. Clear-thinking
8. Jousting spear
9. Masked critter
10. Old Country Store restaurant chain
11. Trout fisherman's wear
12. Affectionate touch
15. Camera bag attachment
18. Deleted, in a way
19. Some small salmons
20. Silly one
21. Shows mercy

DOWN

1. Color similar to lavender
2. Raisin brand
3. Fails, suddenly
4. Light show in the sky
5. Lazy
6. Church singing group
7. Hangs, like an earring
11. Cowboy movie
13. Like adobe
14. Protege's adviser
16. The bounding main
17. Ants at a picnic, e.g.

Answers on page 192.

MOTLEY MIX

ACROSS

1. Flattery
5. Cubes in miso soup
8. "Newsy" SNL segment
9. Royal with a golden touch
12. Canine's coat?
13. Tar's bag
15. Corfu or Crete
18. Divine protector
19. Monopoly card
20. Has the final turn

DOWN

1. Seed scatterer
2. Brandish, as biceps
3. Early look
4. Fervent
6. Switch positions
7. Knife, fork or spoon
10. Iconic Disney symbol
11. Competitive demeanor
12. Betrothed
14. Italian cheese similar to Parmesan
16. Car parker
17. Pearl Mosque site

Answers on page 192.

ANSWERS

Mishmash (page 4)

Grid answers:
- POSEURS / EDEN
- AUNL / SOU
- RIPOSTE / EASEL
- SRUE / ASL
- LEAANDPERRINS
- EGY / SE
- YAMAHA / SCARAB
- OE / SA / U
- SABERRATTLING
- TBO / TANE
- ERODE / FALLGUY
- ASS / SO / OO / OE
- MASS / RIGHTED

Hodgepodge (page 8)

Grid answers:
- BRACELET / IMPS
- UPT / N / AO
- MARGINOFERROR
- SIQR / IT
- OWL / USMARINES
- UFE / EIE
- TOOKTO / EDAMES
- OT / REA / AC
- CULDESACS / MIA
- US / TH / MR
- LADYOFTHELAKE
- TA / ARL / U
- STYX / ITADDSUP

Grab Bag (page 6)

Grid answers:
- SUSPEND / SEPIA
- ELD / EK / AG
- WRING / THINNER
- UP / AA / PDE
- PAPERAIRPLANE
- EA / NI / O
- CIRCLE / UNSEEN
- LL / I / G / X
- ALPHAANDOMEGA
- SEN / FUCC
- SHAMPOO / TOUCH
- ER / OR / OTE
- SOLVE / MANNERS

Common Phrases (page 10)

Grid answers:
- STACCATO / OWES
- PNLH / AU
- ODD / ACROPOLIS
- OER / OK / P
- FASHIONPOLICE
- NEINC
- MINUET / PLIGHT
- OET / DT
- NECESSARYEVIL
- TK / YCII
- ANTIPASTO / RAM
- NI / POGI
- AMEN / RAINCOAT

ANSWERS

Random Knowledge (page 12)

Quiz Time (page 16)

Trivia (page 14)

Small Talk (page 18)

ANSWERS

Crossword Curiosity (page 20)

Melange (page 24)

General Knowledge (page 22)

Quiz Show (page 26)

ANSWERS

Clue Collection (page 28)

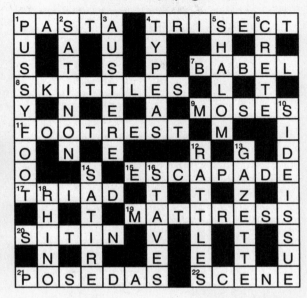

Miscellany (page 32)

Oddments (page 30)

Many M's (page 34)

ANSWERS

In the Books (page 36)

Two from Mythology (page 40)

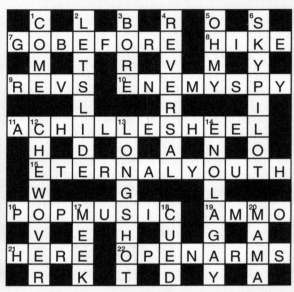

In Print (page 38)

Smorgasbord (page 42)

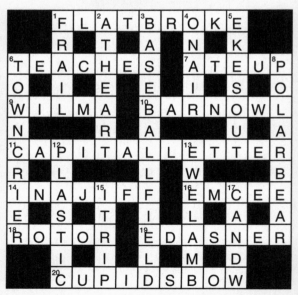

ANSWERS

Friendship and Fire (page 44)

Across answers: AU PAIR · YOU BET · PRACTICAL JOKE · EASY WIN · I'M OFF · IN BLOSSOM · ACHOO · MACH TWO · STICK TOGETHER · TIE UPS · GOES BY

Whatnots (page 48)

Across answers: SPAN · HOT MEALS · NAIVETE · EXPEL · AWESOME SAUCE · COYOTE · EDISON · TAKE YOUR TIME · SIMBA · EMERALD · RUN SLATE · FOXY

Metal and Cloth (page 46)

Across answers: AMPED UP · TUNIC · BERMUDA SHORTS · LINEN · TIE INTO · MCENROE · HI MOM · BUCKET OF BOLTS · A TEAM · LATER ON

Mouth and Stomach (page 50)

Across answers: WISDOM TOOTH · LET GO · I HAVE IT · STAND UP · DRANK · CALL ON · IN A BIT · ENDED · HIT HOME · SIR JOHN · GRETA · GUT RESPONSE

ANSWERS

In Photo and Print (page 52)

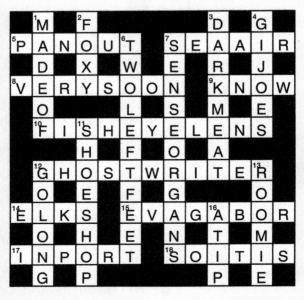

X Marks the Spot (page 56)

To-Do List (page 54)

War, Music, and Theories (page 58)

ANSWERS

Buckets of B's (page 60)

Across answers visible in grid:
BUCKETSEATS, BARSOAP, INLAW, DUEL, GOSOFT, GROWUP, WEIRDO, EVENIF, BYME, IWISH, PSANDQS, DROPTHEBALL

Food and Drink (page 64)

LIPREADS, SPEW, FANBELT, QANDA, HOTPOTATOES, HOLDIT, ATEASE, THEDEMONRUM, UDALL, TWOTIME, SAKE, LOVENEST

Intelligence and Knowledge (page 62)

SPEAKUP, AMUSE, WISPY, STAYPUT, IDIOTSAVANT, FACTCHECKER, POOLCUE, LOCAL, TRINI, KEYRING

Crossword at Capacity (page 66)

HINTED, REPORTER, LEE, DENIAL, CHEM, THEME, SEMINAR, STARTER, ENJOY, WING, AUSTEN, GEL, RINGTONE, TOWERS

ANSWERS

Figurative Phrases (page 68)

The grid spells out, among others: VEGOUT, FARCRY, CZAR, LIEAWAKE, STONESTHROW, THEHAVENOTS, LEFTHOME, GUNS, TUTTUT, TRAGIC

Sink and a Drink (page 72)

The grid spells out, among others: HOTSAUCE, SCOT, GOODEYE, ORING, SOHO, LEADPIPE, GOTOTHEBOTTOM, STARTREK, SKIP, VENUS, TOOSOON, NOMO, DEADSTOP

Keeping Quiet (page 70)

The grid spells out, among others: URGEON, NODICE, UNDERCOVERCOP, SIGNOUT, ADDON, DRDRE, VOTESIN, VEILOFSECRECY, ICEAGE, BETCHA

Familiar Phrases (page 74)

The grid spells out, among others: ATDAWN, POPART, RUNFOR, STOOGE, FAMILIARFACES, EMPATHY, INSOMANYWORDS, TOOTOO, COPIED, PATCHY, VSIGNS

ANSWERS

ABC, Apple, Ball, Crab (page 76)

Air and Space (page 80)

Clue Stew (page 78)

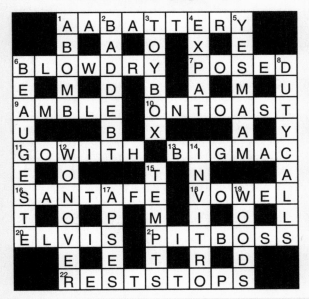

Lots of B's (page 82)

ANSWERS

In the Wild (page 84)

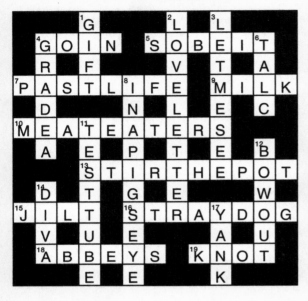

An Ocular Puzzle (page 88)

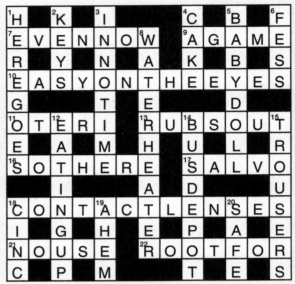

Merry Medley (page 86)

Take a Chance (page 90)

ANSWERS

From Face to Feet (page 92)

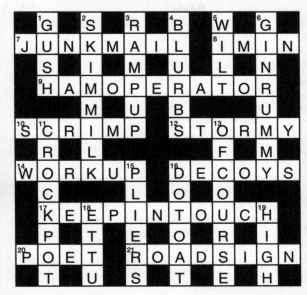

Across answers include:
LAKEBED, CUBES, ADIEU, GOODGUY, HAIRSTYLIST, ABBOT, USHER, BRAKELIGHTS, CLIPART, ETAIL, THEME, DRSEUSS

Written and Spoken (page 96)

JUNKMAIL, IMIN, HAMOPERATOR, SCRIMP, STORMY, WORKUP, DECOYS, KEEPINTOUCH, POET, ROADSIGN

Clue Accumulation (page 94)

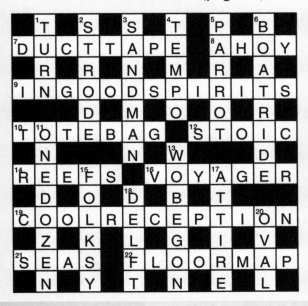

DUCTTAPE, AHOY, INGOODSPIRITS, TOTEBAG, STOIC, REEFS, VOYAGER, COOLRECEPTION, SEAS, FLOORMAP

Curious Crossword (page 98)

BOPEEP, HEEHAW, DEARJOHN, LAOS, NOTHINGTOIT, JUSTASECOND, ETTA, SMALLFRY, DETAIN, ENZYME

183

ANSWERS

A Phrase and a Song (page 100)

Stories and Music (page 104)

Decisions and Questions (page 102)

Collectibles and Precious Things (page 106)

ANSWERS

Tools and Gems (page 108)

1 H	2 A	V	3 E	A	4 C	O	5 W	■	6 P	A	7 C	K
■	R	■	L	■	U	■	A	■	R	■	O	■
8 F	E	T	E	■	9 R	I	N	S	E	O	U	T
■	S	■	C	■	L	■	D	■	C	■	N	■
10 N	O	R	T	H	S	E	A	■	11 I	O	T	A
■	■	■	R	■	U	■	■	■	O	■	O	■
■	12 H	A	I	R	P	I	13 N	T	U	R	N	■
■	O	■	C	■	■	■	A	■	S	■	■	■
14 A	G	E	D	■	15 B	A	N	K	S	H	16 O	T
■	W	■	R	■	R	■	E	■	T	■	T	■
17 M	A	G	I	C	A	C	T	■	18 O	B	E	Y
■	S	■	L	■	S	■	T	■	N	■	R	■
19 P	H	I	L	■	20 S	H	E	D	E	V	I	L

Tuneful Phrases (page 112)

■	1 L	■	■	■	2 G	■	3 F	■	■	■	4 Q	■
5 B	O	O	6 B	O	O	■	7 I	N	8 F	L	U	X
■	W	■	A	■	G	■	R	■	A	■	I	■
■	9 C	A	N	N	E	D	M	U	S	I	C	■
■	A	■	A	■	T	■	■	■	T	■	H	■
10 F	L	A	N	■	11 T	O	12 L	L	F	R	E	E
■	■	■	A	■	E	■	I	■	O	■	■	■
13 P	14 R	E	S	E	R	V	E	■	15 R	I	16 S	K
■	O	■	P	■	■	■	S	■	W	■	I	■
■	17 A	L	L	T	18 H	A	T	J	A	Z	Z	■
■	M	■	I	■	O	■	I	■	R	■	E	■
19 K	E	P	T	O	N	■	20 L	U	D	L	U	M
■	D	■	■	■	K	■	L	■	■	■	P	■

A Bit of Wordplay (page 110)

1 H	A	2 N	S	3 O	L	4 O	■	5 D	E	6 P	O	7 T
U	■	I	■	F	■	L	■	O	■	U	■	H
8 G	C	L	E	F	■	9 D	O	G	S	T	A	R
E	■	E	■	Y	■	I	■	M	■	T	■	E
■	■	■	■	10 E	A	S	Y	A	S	P	I	E
11 P	■	12 I	■	A	■	H	■	■	■	U	■	W
13 R	A	N	D	R	Y	■	14 A	15 G	A	T	H	A
E	■	N	■	■	■	16 U	■	E	■	T	■	Y
17 S	M	E	L	18 L	A	R	A	T	■	■	■	■
S	■	R	■	A	■	G	■	E	■	19 I	■	20 G
21 B	R	E	A	T	H	E	■	22 V	J	D	A	Y
O	■	A	■	E	■	N	■	E	■	E	■	M
23 X	E	R	O	X	■	24 T	I	N	C	A	N	S

Test Your Knowledge (page 114)

■	1 I	■	2 L	■	3 G	■	4 I	■	5 H	■	6 F	■
7 M	A	D	E	D	O	■	8 S	T	I	V	E	S
■	M	■	T	■	O	■	L	■	T	■	E	■
■	9 B	L	O	O	D	V	E	S	S	E	L	■
■	■	■	U	■	N	■	■	■	O	■	F	■
10 S	11 P	A	T	■	12 A	R	13 M	I	N	A	R	M
■	L	■	■	■	M	■	A	■	■	■	E	■
14 B	A	D	15 B	R	E	A	K	■	16 T	R	E	K
■	Y	■	E	■	■	■	E	■	O	■	■	■
■	17 F	U	D	G	18 E	R	I	P	P	L	19 E	■
■	A	■	B	■	A	■	T	■	D	■	V	■
20 P	I	N	U	P	S	■	21 S	T	O	W	I	T
■	R	■	G	■	Y	■	O	■	G	■	L	■

ANSWERS

Best Time for a Party (page 116)

1C	O	2M	M	3A	F	4A	U	5L	T			
A		R		H		R		A		6D		7L
8B	A	C	H	E	L	O	R	P	A	R	T	Y
F		L		A		U		B		N		R
9A	T	E	U	P		10S	T	E	P	O	N	E
R		A				E		L				
11E	R	N	E	12S	T		13S	T	U	14C	C	15O
				W		16S				A		H
17A	I	18R	V	E	N	T		19C	A	R	O	M
R		A		E		O		D		A		S
20T	A	C	I	T	A	P	P	R	O	V	A	L
Y		E		O		I		O		A		A
			21A	N	Y	T	I	M	E	N	O	W

Q Marks the Spot (page 120)

1C	U	2E	B	3A	L	4L		5M	O	6T	I	7F
O		S		B		E		E		Y		E
8P	A	T	T	I		9M	O	O	N	P	I	E
E		E		T		O		W		E		L
10S	A	L	T	M	I	N	E		11W	A	I	F
		L		U		S		12F				O
13F	R	E	N	C	H	Q	U	A	R	14T	E	R
A				H		U		C		A		
15L	A	16I	T		17P	E	T	E	R	P	A	18N
L		M		19T		E		C		I		O
20G	E	E	W	H	I	Z		21A	D	O	U	T
U		A		U		E		R		C		M
22Y	A	N	K	S		23R	E	D	T	A	P	E

Birds and Flowers (page 118)

1B	A	2L	D	3E	A	4G	L	5E	S			
L		U		G		E		R		6B		
7I	N	S	H	O	R	T		8A	W	A	R	9D
P		H		T		M		T		N		R
			10B	R	E	A	K	O	F	D	A	Y
11S		12F		I		D				A		W
13C	R	I	S	P	Y		14B	15I	K	I	N	I
O		G				16S		N		D		T
17W	E	L	L	18I	N	E	V	E	R			
L		E		N		E		R		19M		20O
21S	C	A	L	A		22S	O	R	T	O	U	T
		F		W		T		O		S		I
			23B	E	D	O	F	R	O	S	E	S

Valentine's Day (page 122)

1S		2A		3V				4G		5B		6R
7H	A	U	L	O	F	8F		9O	F	A	G	E
A		G		I		L		T		J		V
10D	A	R	K	C	H	O	C	O	L	A	T	E
O		A		E		R		S				R
11W	I	T	S		12D	I	V	E	B	13O	M	B
		I		14O		D		A		L		
15S	O	N	I	N	L	A	W		16V	I	E	17W
P				B		K		18S		V		I
19H	E	20A	D	O	V	E	R	H	E	E	L	S
I		I		A		Y		E		O		E
21N	A	D	E	R		22S	K	I	L	I	F	T
X		E		D				K		L		O

ANSWERS

A Vacation from Cleaning (page 124)

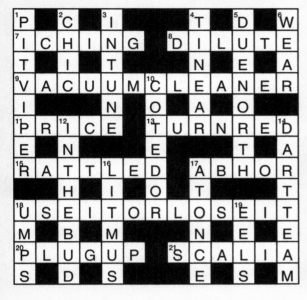

Figurative Places (page 128)

Fun and Games (page 126)

Knowledge Is Power (page 130)

ANSWERS

Around the World (page 132)

Tangled Up (page 136)

Fill in the Phrase (page 134)

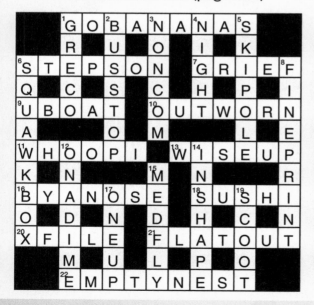

Patchwork (page 138)

ANSWERS

On the Screen or in Nature (page 140)

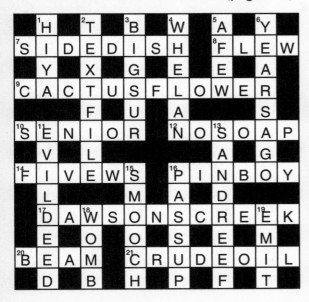

Fresh Batch (page 144)

Ragbag (page 142)

Phrase Assortment (page 146)

ANSWERS

Fantastic Phrases (page 148)

Odds and Ends (page 152)

Classic Crossword (page 150)

Mix It Up (page 154)

ANSWERS

Potpourri (page 156)

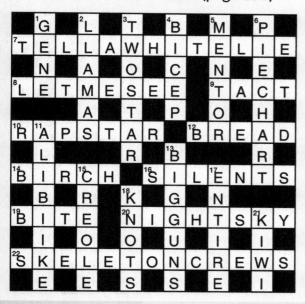

1 C	A	2 S	T	3 L	E	4 S	■	5 I	N	6 E	R	7 T
A	■	Q	■	A	■	H	■	M	■	P	■	O
8 S	A	U	N	T	E	R	■	9 A	M	I	T	Y
E	■	A	■	E	■	O	■	G	■	C	■	S
10 B	A	B	Y	B	O	U	T	I	Q	U	E	■
O	■	■	■	R	■	D	■	N	■	R	■	11 H
12 O	O	13 D	L	E	S	■	14 G	A	Z	E	B	O
K	■	W	■	A	■	15 P	■	R	■	■	■	L
■	16 T	I	C	K	E	R	S	Y	M	17 B	O	L
18 E	■	N	■	F	■	I	■	L	■	A	■	E
19 M	E	D	E	A	■	20 S	P	I	N	N	E	R
M	■	L	■	S	■	M	■	N	■	D	■	A
21 A	V	E	R	T	■	22 S	H	E	R	B	E	T

Cornucopia (page 160)

1 C	H	2 A	I	3 R	L	I	F	4 T	■	5 M	O	6 B
U	■	T	■	A	■	■	■	U	■	O	■	E
7 L	E	O	N	I	N	E	■	8 R	A	N	G	E
D	■	L	■	L	■	■	■	N	■	S	■	F
9 E	N	L	A	R	G	10 E	S	U	P	O	N	■
S	■	■	■	O	■	V	■	P	■	O	■	11 S
A	■	12 B	■	13 A	L	E	U	T	■	N	■	A
C	■	A	■	D	■	N	■	H	■	■	■	M
■	14 C	R	O	S	S	T	H	E	L	15 I	N	E
16 I	■	R	■	P	■	■	■	H	■	P	■	H
17 K	H	A	K	I	■	18 A	N	E	M	O	N	E
E	■	G	■	K	■	■	■	A	■	D	■	R
19 A	C	E	■	20 E	A	S	Y	T	O	S	E	E

Flotsam and Jetsam (page 158)

■	1 G	■	2 L	■	3 T	■	4 B	■	5 M	■	6 P	■
7 T	E	L	L	A	W	H	I	T	E	L	I	E
■	N	■	A	■	O	■	C	■	N	■	E	■
8 L	E	T	M	E	S	E	E	■	9 T	A	C	T
■	■	■	A	■	T	■	P	■	O	■	H	■
10 R	11 A	P	S	T	A	R	■	12 B	R	E	A	D
■	L	■	■	■	R	■	13 B	■	■	■	R	■
14 B	I	R	15 C	H	■	16 S	I	L	17 E	N	T	S
■	B	■	R	■	18 K	■	G	■	N	■	■	■
19 B	I	T	E	■	20 N	I	G	H	T	S	21 K	Y
■	I	■	O	■	O	■	U	■	I	■	I	■
22 S	K	E	L	E	T	O	N	C	R	E	W	S
■	E	■	E	■	S	■	S	■	E	■	I	■

Panoply (page 162)

■	1 M	■	2 C	■	3 B	■	4 U	■	5 S	■	6 U	■
7 M	U	S	E	U	M	■	8 S	C	H	E	M	E
■	M	■	L	■	O	■	U	■	R	■	P	■
9 O	B	I	S	■	10 V	E	R	B	A	T	I	M
■	A	■	■	■	I	■	P	■	P	■	R	■
11 P	I	E	12 R	C	E	S	■	13 S	N	E	E	R
■	■	■	A	■	S	■	14 B	■	E	■	■	■
15 S	16 K	A	T	E	■	17 L	U	L	L	A	18 B	Y
■	V	■	E	■	19 L	■	R	■	■	■	O	■
20 T	E	A	C	H	I	N	G	■	21 O	K	O	K
■	T	■	U	■	G	■	L	■	G	■	B	■
22 S	C	O	T	C	H	■	23 A	I	R	L	O	G
■	H	■	S	■	T	■	R	■	E	■	O	■

ANSWERS

Knickknacks (page 164)

Doodads (page 168)

Jumble (page 166)

Motley Mix (page 170)